Big and Small, Room for All

Jo Ellen Bogart

Illustrated by Gillian Newland

TUNDRA BOOKS

Published in Canada by Tundra Books,
75 Sherbourne Street, Toronto, Ontario M5A 2P9

Published in the United States by Tundra Books of Northern
New York, P.O. Box 1030, Plattsburgh, New York 12901

Library of Congress Control Number: 2008903009

Medium: watercolor on paper

Design: Leah Springate

Printed in Singapore

1 2 3 4 5 6   14 13 12 11 10 09

Library and Archives Canada Cataloguing in Publication

Bogart, Jo Ellen, 1945-
    Big and small, room for all / Jo Ellen Bogart ; Gillian Newland,
illustrator.

ISBN 978-0-88776-891-0 (bound)

    1. Size judgment – Juvenile literature. 2. Size perception –
Juvenile literature. I. Newland, Gillian II. Title.

BF299.S5B64 2009   j153.7'52   C2008-902062-6

We acknowledge the financial support of the Government of Canada
through the Book Publishing Industry Development Program
(BPIDP) and that of the Government of Ontario through the Ontario
Media Development Corporation's Ontario Book Initiative. We
further acknowledge the support of the Canada Council for the Arts
and the Ontario Arts Council for our publishing program.

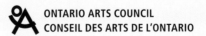

ONTARIO ARTS COUNCIL
CONSEIL DES ARTS DE L'ONTARIO

For my darling grandson, Milo

J.E.B.

For my friends and family, and for B, for all your love and support

G.N.

Big and small,
Big and small

Room for all,
Big and small

Big sky,
Small Sun

Big Sun,
Small Earth

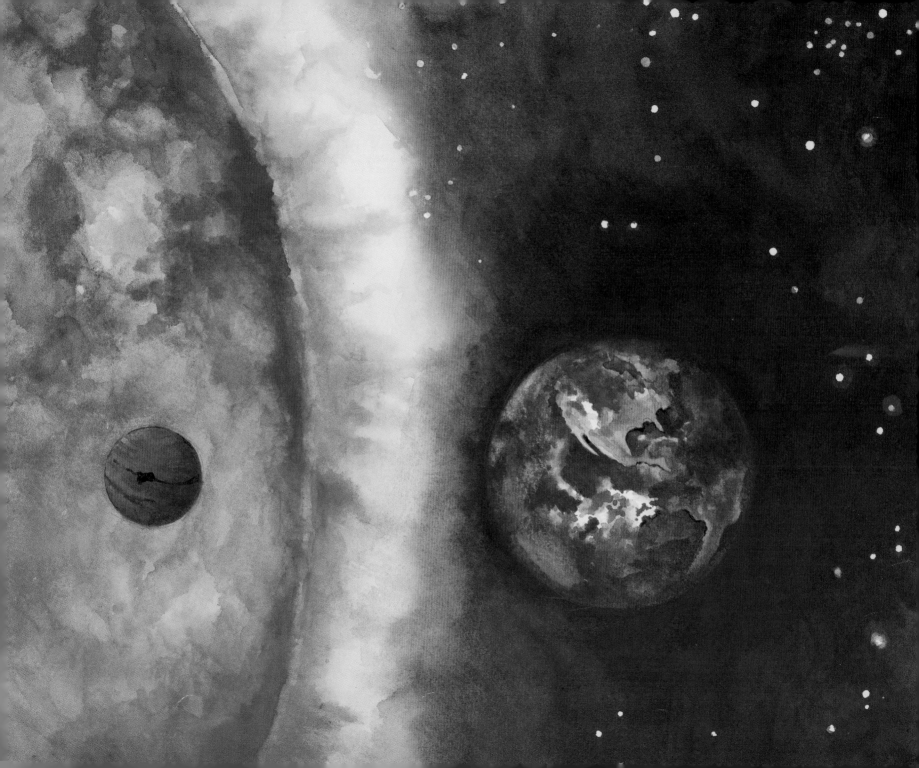

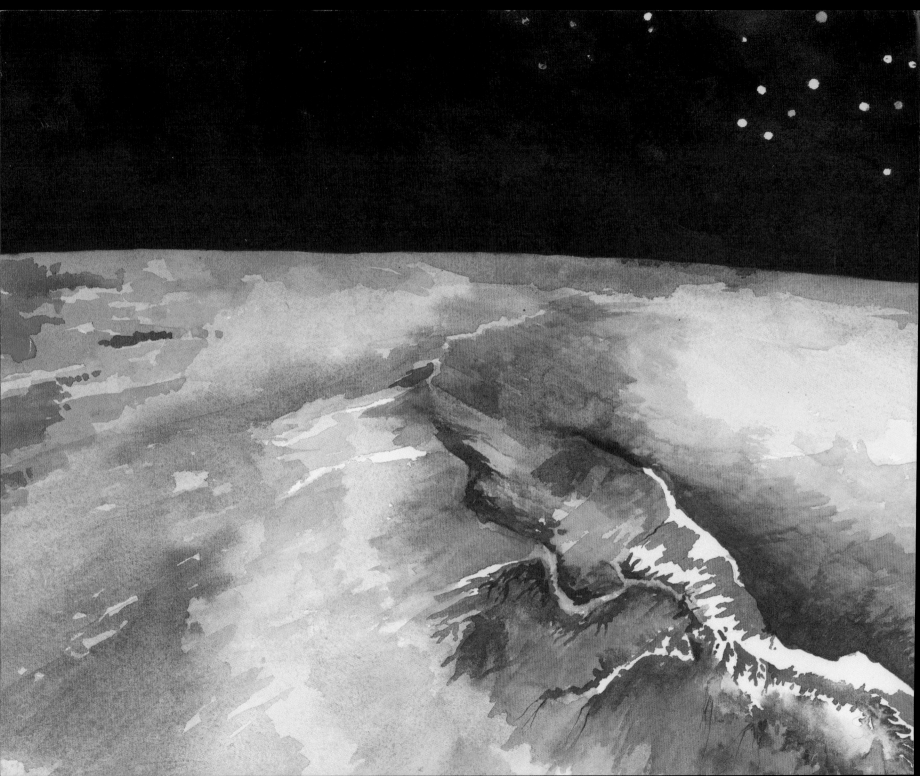

Big Earth,
Small mountain

Big mountain,
Small tree

Big tree,

Small man

Big man,
Small child

Big child,
Small kitten

Big kitten,
Small mouse

Big mouse,
Small flea

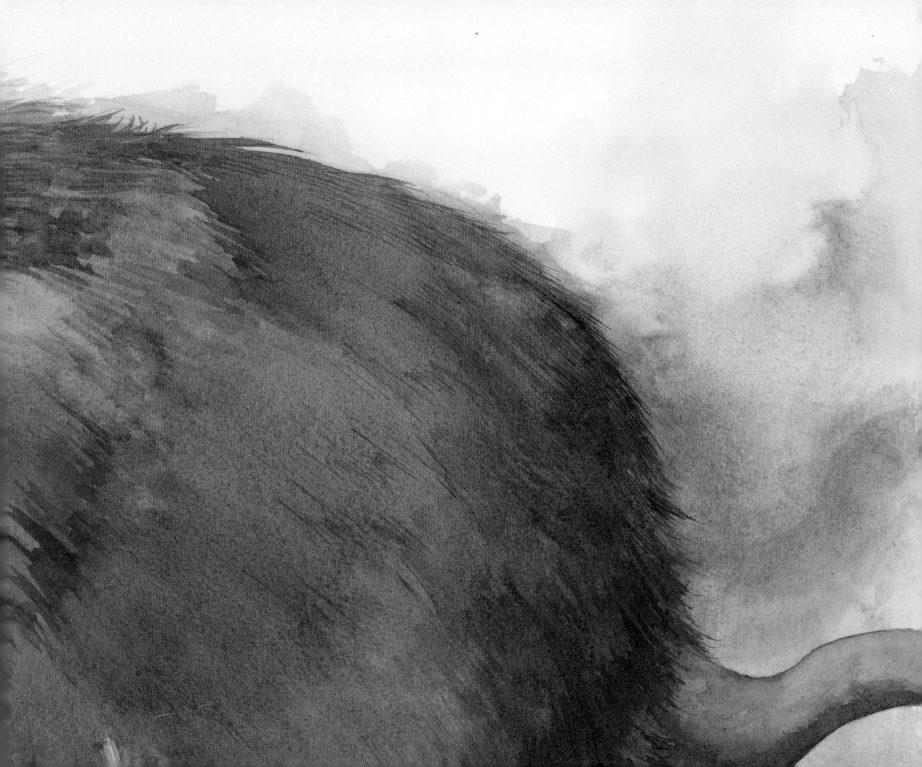

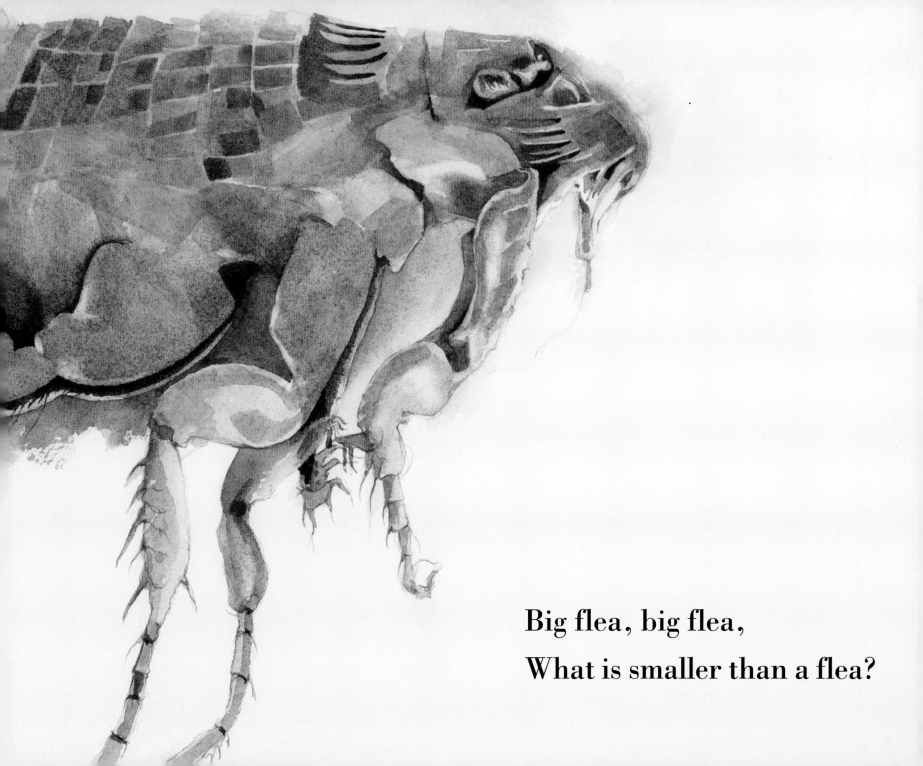

Big flea, big flea,

What is smaller than a flea?

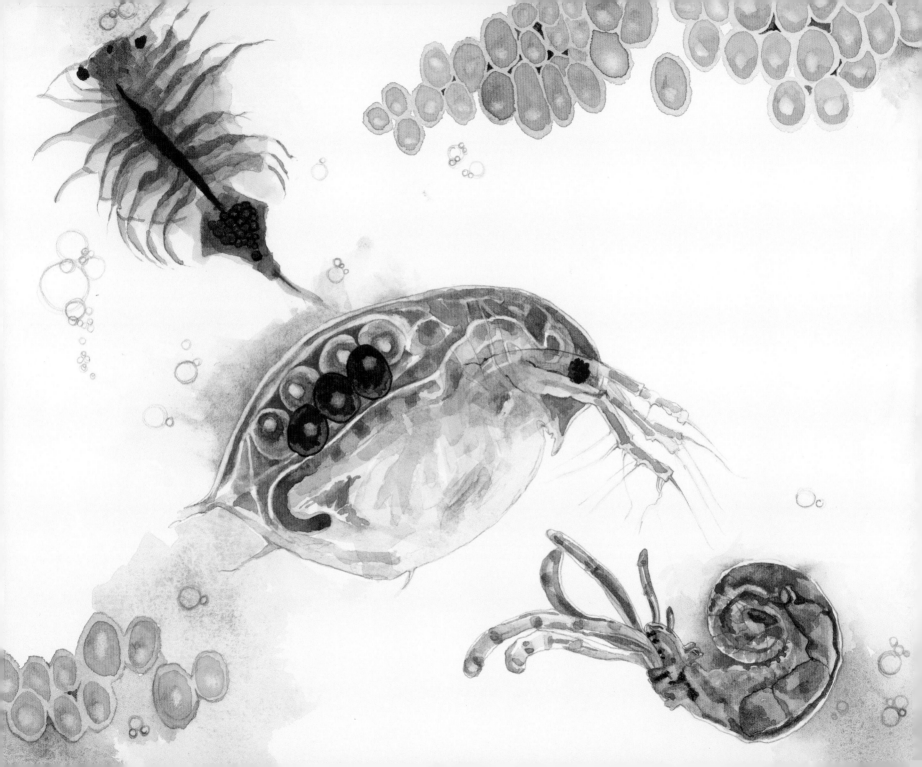

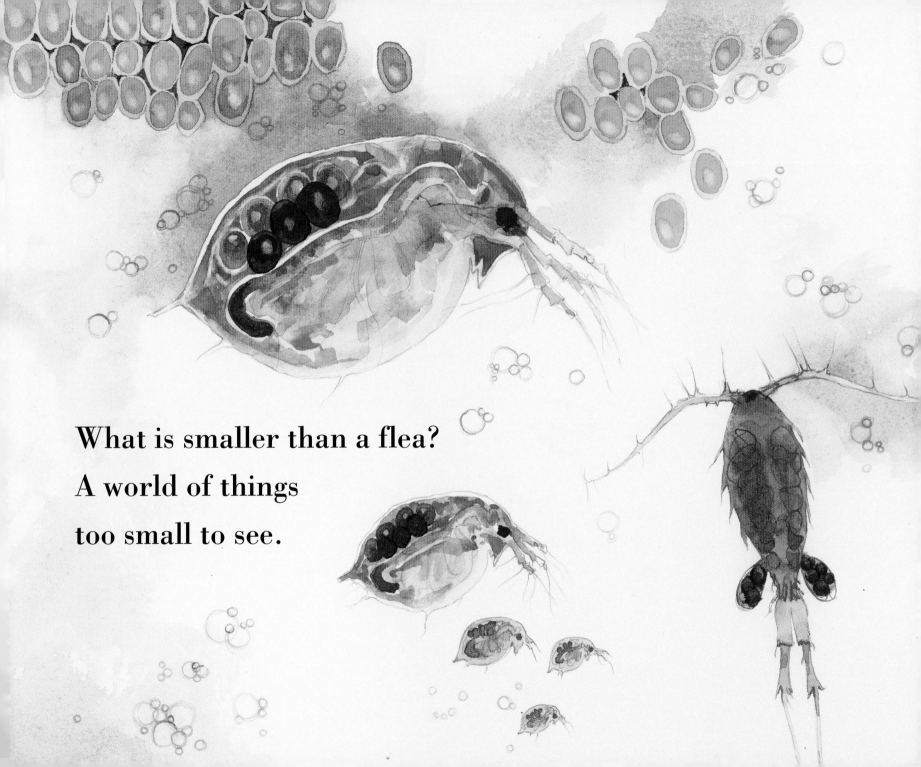

What is smaller than a flea?
A world of things
too small to see.

Big sky, big sky,
What is bigger
than the sky?

What is bigger than the sky?
The never-ever-ending sky.